AUBURN TIGERS

BY

RAMEY TEMPLE

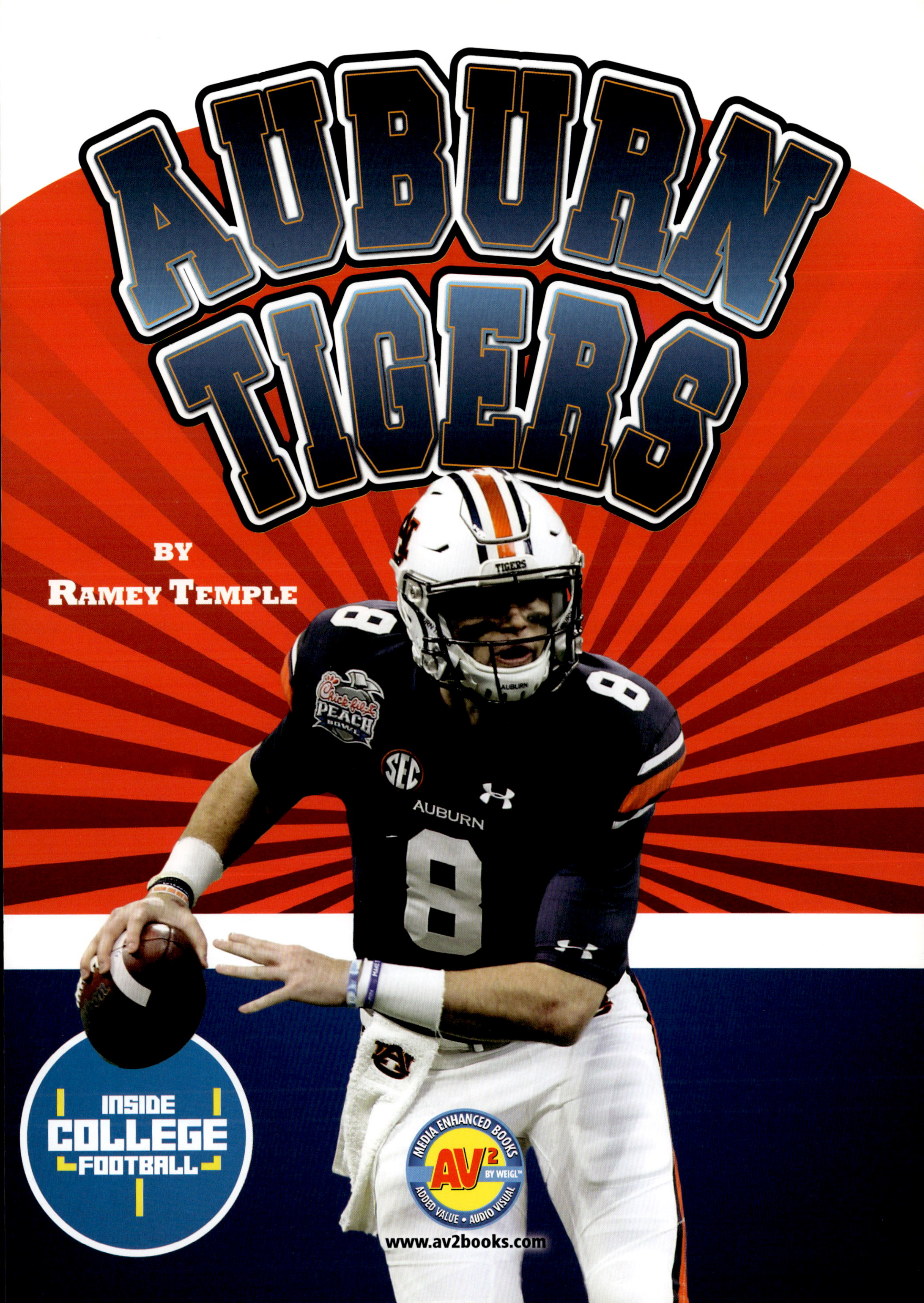

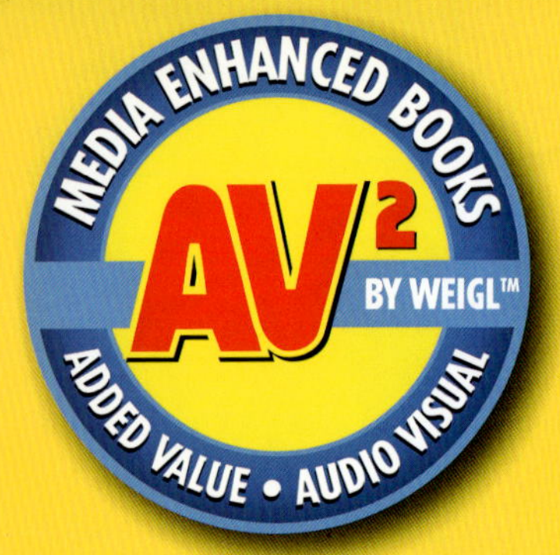

Go to **www.av2books.com**, and enter this book's unique code.

BOOK CODE

AVT52822

AV² by Weigl brings you media enhanced books that support active learning.

AV² provides enriched content that supplements and complements this book. Weigl's AV² books strive to create inspired learning and engage young minds in a total learning experience.

Your AV² Media Enhanced books come alive with...

Audio
Listen to sections of the book read aloud.

Key Words
Study vocabulary, and complete a matching word activity.

Video
Watch informative video clips.

Quizzes
Test your knowledge.

Embedded Weblinks
Gain additional information for research.

Slideshow
View images and captions, and prepare a presentation.

Try This!
Complete activities and hands-on experiments.

... and much, much more!

Published by AV² by Weigl
350 5th Avenue, 59th Floor
New York, NY 10118
Website: www.av2books.com

Library of Congress Control Number: 2018968207

ISBN 978-1-7911-0084-1 (hardcover)
ISBN 978-1-7911-0085-8 (multi-user eBook)
ISBN 978-1-7911-0086-5 (single-user eBook)

Printed in Guangzhou, China
1 2 3 4 5 6 7 8 9 0 23 22 21 20 19

042019
102318

Project Coordinator: Jared Siemens   Designer: Terry Paulhus

Every reasonable effort has been made to trace ownership and to obtain permission to reprint copyright material. The publishers would be pleased to have any errors or omissions brought to their attention so that they may be corrected in subsequent printings.

The publisher acknowledges Alamy, Getty Images, and Wikimedia Commons as its primary image suppliers for this title.

Auburn Tigers

CONTENTS

Introduction

The Auburn Tigers are a powerhouse football program. They have had more than 10 undefeated seasons and have won more than 700 games. Successful coaches and strong **National Championship** teams have defined their history.

Auburn began its football program prior to the 1900s. It was one of the founding members of the Southeastern Conference (SEC) in 1933. Auburn has many traditions that are a part of its rich football heritage. The Iron Bowl is an example of this. It is an annual game played between Auburn and another SEC team, the University of Alabama Crimson Tide. The Iron Bowl is one of college football's biggest **rivalries**.

Auburn running back Kerryon Johnson led the SEC in carries, rushing yards, rushing touchdowns, and total touchdowns in the 2017 season.

The Tigers have produced three **Heisman Memorial Trophy** winners and 12 College Football **Hall of Famers**. Quarterback Cam Newton and running back Bo Jackson are just two examples of the talent that has been recruited by Auburn. Auburn helped develop these players into the National Football League (NFL) stars they became.

Darius James earned a starting position with Auburn in 2016 and was named third-team All-SEC for his defensive contributions during the 2017 season.

AUBURN

Stadium Jordan-Hare Stadium

Division Southeastern Conference (SEC) Western

Head Coach Gus Malzahn

Location Auburn, Alabama

National Championships 2

Nicknames The Tigers

26 Head Coaches

43 Bowl Game Appearances

3 Heisman Trophy Winners

12 Conference Championships

History

Twelve Tigers coaches and players have been inducted into the **College Football Hall of Fame.**

Coach Tommy Tuberville and the Auburn Tigers defeated the University of Tennessee Volunteers 38–28 to secure the 2004 SEC championship.

The Auburn Tigers played their first football game in 1892. The Tigers' first full-time head coach was John Heisman. He helped establish the football program, and the locals took notice. By 1939, Drake Field could not hold the large crowds, so the university built the Auburn Stadium for the Tigers.

One of Auburn's most famous coaches, Ralph "Shug" Jordan, was hired in 1951. Six years later, he led the Tigers to an undefeated season and the National Championship. Jordan coached quarterback Pat Sullivan, the team's first Heisman Trophy winner. After some mediocre years, Coach Pat Dye was hired in 1981 to help the team get back to its former glory. From 1981 to 1992, the Tigers won four SEC championships, and Bo Jackson won the team's second Heisman.

The 2004 season was a great one for the Tigers. They won the SEC championship, the Sugar Bowl, and had another undefeated season. With the help of team leaders Cam Newton and Nick Fairley, they won their second National Championship in 2010. Also in 2010, Newton won the team's third Heisman. Head coach Gus Malzahn was hired in 2013. In his first year of coaching, the Tigers won both their division and their conference championships.

The Auburn football team was founded by history and Latin professor George Petrie. Petrie picked the team's orange and blue colors because of his time at the University of Virginia, whose colors are also orange and blue.

The Stadium

Although the University of Alabama's stadium is now larger, the energy of nearly 90,000 fans cheering on the Tigers makes Jordan-Hare Stadium one of college football's most intimidating venues.

When Auburn Stadium opened in 1939, it was considered **state-of-the-art**. The small city of Auburn was proud to have a stadium that rivaled other SEC football fields. It had 7,500 seats and was a great improvement from the prior playing field.

The Tigers' stadium has gone through many name changes. In 1949, the stadium name was changed to Cliff Hare Stadium. Clifford Hare played on Auburn's very first football team and was president of the Southern Conference, which later became the SEC. The stadium name changed again in 1973 to Jordan-Hare Stadium. This name recognized Coach "Shug" Jordan, Auburn's all-time winningest coach. In 2005, the Tigers decided to name the field of play. They called it Pat Dye Field, after one of Auburn's most successful head coaches.

Jordan-Hare Stadium has been expanded five different times. Some of the additions include luxury suites, press boxes, and a high-definition scoreboard. The stadium can now hold more than 80,000 people. It has been said that when the Tigers play a home game, Jordan-Hare Stadium becomes Alabama's fifth-largest city.

One of the most unique traditions at Jordan-Hare Stadium is the flight of Auburn's "War Eagle," a golden eagle named Nova. Nova flies around the entire stadium and lands at midfield before every home football game.

Where They Play

Welcome to Jordan-Hare Stadium, where more than 87,000 Auburn fans gather to watch the Tigers compete on Pat Dye Field. Fans are surrounded by displays of blue and orange. Current and former Auburn players and students continue to return to the stadium to cheer during home games.

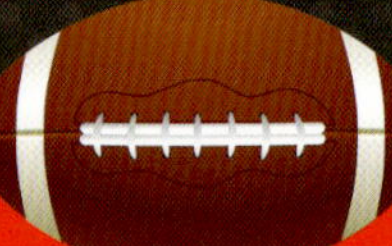

SEC WEST

★ 1 **Auburn University**
Auburn, Alabama

2 **Louisiana State University**
Baton Rouge, Louisiana

3 **Mississippi State University**
Starkville, Mississippi

4 **Texas A&M University**
College Station, Texas

5 **University of Alabama**
Tuscaloosa, Alabama

6 **University of Arkansas**
Fayetteville, Arkansas

7 **University of Mississippi**
Oxford, Mississippi

Arena
Jordan-Hare Stadium

Location
Auburn, Alabama

Broke Ground
1939

Completed
November 30, 1939

Surface
Real Grass

Features
- East-side exterior features murals of great plays and players from Auburn's history
- Seating capacity of 87,451
- Tenth largest on-campus stadium in the United States

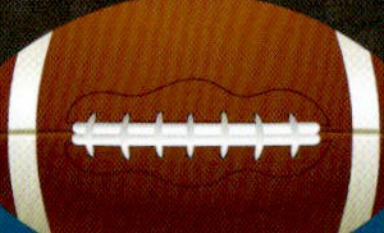

SEC EAST

1 **University of Florida**
Gainesville, Florida

2 **University of Georgia**
Athens, Georgia

3 **University of Kentucky**
Lexington, Kentucky

4 **University of Missouri**
Columbia, Missouri

5 **University of South Carolina**
Columbia, South Carolina

6 **University of Tennessee**
Knoxville, Tennessee

7 **Vanderbilt University**
Nashville, Tennessee

NORTH DAKOTA
SOUTH DAKOTA
NEBRASKA
KANSAS
OKLAHOMA
TEXAS
MINNESOTA
IOWA
MISSOURI
ARKANSAS
LOUISIANA
WISCONSIN
ILLINOIS
MISSISSIPPI
MICHIGAN
INDIANA
KENTUCKY
TENNESSEE
ALABAMA
OHIO
WEST VIRGINIA
VIRGINIA
NORTH CAROLINA
SOUTH CAROLINA
GEORGIA
FLORIDA
PENNSYLVANIA
NEW YORK
NEW HAMPSHIRE
VERMONT
MAINE
MASSACHUSETTS
RHODE ISLAND
CONNECTICUT
NEW JERSEY
DELAWARE
MARYLAND
WASHINGTON, D.C.
Atlantic Ocean
Gulf of Mexico
1
2
3
4
5
6
7
SCALE
0 miles
500 miles
0 kilometers
500 km
LEGEND
Home Stadium
SEC West
SEC East
United States
Other Countries
Water

The Uniforms

Beginning in the **2017** season, Auburn added **3D bumpers** to the front of their helmets. The bumpers say "TIGERS."

Auburn's uniforms were ranked the 17th best in college football by NBC Sports going into the 2018 season. The Tigers' traditional look is a fan and media favorite.

In the early years, the Tiger uniform changed often. However, it usually consisted of varying combinations of orange and navy blue. In 1929, the Tigers tried something different and wore a white jersey with an orange tiger head. That did not last long, though. The Tigers went back to their faithful orange and blue. The general look of the current-day uniforms began in 1957, the year Auburn won the National Championship.

HOME

AWAY

Today's Auburn Tigers uniform is made up of white pants with orange and blue stripes. The players wear either a blue jersey with orange and white stripes on the shoulder or a white jersey with orange and blue stripes. The helmets are white with orange and blue stripes. An interlocking AU for Auburn University is on the helmets. There have not been any big changes to the uniforms recently, only minor adjustments, such as adding different helmet decals. The Tigers' uniforms are made by Under Armour.

The Tigers' helmets have been white since the early 1950s, and the AU logo became a helmet staple in 1966 when it replaced player numbers.

Student Athletes

Approximately **60 percent of Auburn freshmen** are awarded a scholarship.

In 2017, starting quarterback Jarrett Stidham threw for 3,158 yards and 18 touchdowns during his first season with Auburn. Stidham decided to leave Auburn after his junior year in hopes of playing in the NFL.

Being a college student athlete is hard work. Athletes have to perform on the football field and in the classroom. Auburn student athletes are required to meet a minimum grade point average and attend all of their classes. They must also earn 12 academic credits per term. Auburn student athletes have access to Student-Athlete Support Services. Every Auburn student athlete is also assigned to an athletics academic counselor.

Many student athletes are given athletic scholarships. An athletic scholarship is a financial aid agreement between the athlete and the college. Athletes who do not receive scholarships can also be "walk-on" members of the team. This means they are on the team, but without athletic financial aid. Auburn typically awards the maximum number of football scholarships allowed, which is 85. The rest of the team is comprised of walk-ons.

Running back Malik Miller competed with veteran teammates and battled multiple injuries to earn regular time on the field during Auburn's 2018 season.

Bowl Games

The Tigers played their **first bowl game** in 1937 when an exhibition game was hosted in Havana, Cuba.

The Auburn Tigers were victorious against the Purdue Boilermakers in the 2018 Franklin American Mortgage Company Music City Bowl. The Tigers defeated Purdue 63–14 and set a bowl record for most points scored in any half of a bowl game.

After the college football season ends, a rare sports tradition begins. There is no National Collegiate Athletic Association (NCAA)-sponsored **postseason** for the sport of football. Instead, a variety of games called bowl games are played. There are currently 40 bowl games played between college football teams. These games give teams the chance to play rivals or new teams. They are also a chance to compete for respect and wins even after the teams have finished with the regular season.

The Tigers have played in more than 40 bowl games. They have played both the Gator Bowl and the Sugar Bowl six times each. The Tigers' bowl game record is 24–17–2. They also play in an annual game called the Iron Bowl, which is not technically a bowl game. This game is played during their regular season against their biggest foe, Alabama.

In Auburn's 2013 Iron Bowl defeat of Alabama, the Crimson Tide missed a game-winning 57-yard field goal attempt. Tigers cornerback Chris Davis caught the ball and ran in a 109-yard touchdown to seal Auburn's victory.

The Coaches

Current Auburn head coach Gus Malzahn led the Tigers to their eighth SEC title and a National Championship game in 2013. Malzahn received seven awards for his efforts, including the Paul "Bear" Bryant Award and the Associated Press College Football Coach of the Year Award.

Auburn University has been the home to several **prominent** football coaches. John Heisman was one of the team's first coaches. A football player himself, he helped to legalize the forward pass that is now central to the game of football. Ralph "Shug" Jordan took over in the 1950s and remained the head coach for 25 years.

JOHN HEISMAN John Heisman was the Auburn head coach for five seasons from 1895 to 1899. He was the university's fifth head football coach. There is a **bust** of Coach Heisman at Jordan-Hare Stadium. Heisman's record at Auburn was 12–4–2. After coaching at Auburn, he went on to coach several other college football teams.

RALPH "SHUG" JORDAN "Shug" Jordan was the winningest coach in Auburn history. During his time as coach from 1951 to 1975, the Tigers went to 12 bowl games and won the 1957 National Championship. Jordan also coached the team during an impressive 24-game winning streak. In 1957, Jordan was voted National Coach of the Year. His record at Auburn was 176–83–6.

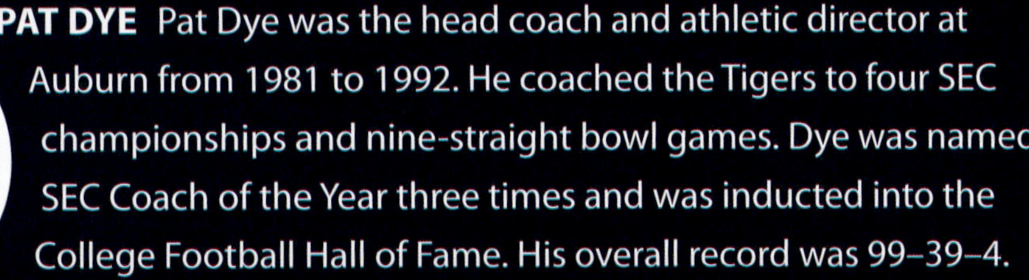

PAT DYE Pat Dye was the head coach and athletic director at Auburn from 1981 to 1992. He coached the Tigers to four SEC championships and nine-straight bowl games. Dye was named SEC Coach of the Year three times and was inducted into the College Football Hall of Fame. His overall record was 99–39–4.

The Mascot

When he is not riding his moped, Aubie the Tiger can be seen on the sidelines at Jordan-Hare Stadium. Aubie wears a number one jersey and carries an Auburn flag or waves a giant foam finger to pump up the crowd.

Auburn University's official mascot is named Aubie the Tiger. He is an Auburn student in a tiger costume. Aubie began as a cartoon character who first appeared on an Auburn football program cover on October 3, 1959. The cartoon tiger was created by Phil Neel, a *Birmingham-Post Herald* artist.

Aubie made his mascot debut in 1979 at an Auburn basketball game. Over the years, Aubie has wowed the fans with his enthusiasm and mix of both tiger and human traits. Aubie has won many awards. He won the Mascot National Championship a record nine times and has been inducted into the Mascot Hall of Fame. In 2014, Aubie won the Capital One Mascot of the Year award.

Auburn students who share the responsibility of playing Aubie the Tiger are called "Friends of Aubie." Friends of Aubie must go through a difficult three-part tryout process, attend classes about how to portray Aubie, and agree to live in Auburn during the summer if they are chosen.

Legends of the Past

For many players, their time with the Tigers is the start of a promising football career. These are some of the best-known football players to play for Auburn University.

Cam Newton

Cam Newton played for one season at Auburn before going pro. As starting quarterback, he led the Tigers to the 2010 National Championship and won the Heisman Trophy. Newton was also voted the SEC Player of the Year and the AP Player of the Year. He was the first pick in the 2011 NFL **draft** by the Carolina Panthers. Newton has gone on to become one of the NFL's major stars. In 2015, Newton helped lead the Panthers to an impressive 15–1 season. That year, the Panthers made it to the Super Bowl and Newton won the NFL **Most Valuable Player (MVP)** award.

Position: Quarterback
Seasons: 2010 (Auburn Tigers), 2011–Present (Carolina Panthers)
Born: May 11, 1989, Atlanta, Georgia

Bo Jackson

Bo Jackson is considered one of the most talented athletes of all time. Right out of high school, Jackson was drafted by the New York Yankees to play baseball, but he chose to go to Auburn and play football instead. During his time at Auburn, he was a two-time Consensus All-American and won the Heisman Trophy. After Auburn, he played professional baseball. He was then drafted by the Los Angeles Raiders in the 1987 NFL draft and played both professional baseball and football at the same time. Jackson had a football career-ending injury at the end of his 1990 season. He retired from all pro sports in 1995.

Position: Running Back
Seasons: 1982–1985 (Auburn Tigers), 1987–1990 (Los Angeles Raiders)
Born: November 30, 1962, Bessemer, Alabama

Pat Sullivan

Pat Sullivan was one of Auburn's greatest players. Playing under Coach Jordan, Sullivan was named SEC Player of the Year twice and was the MVP in two bowl games. He won a Heisman Trophy, and his name is still in the Auburn record books. Sullivan was a second-round draft pick by the Atlanta Falcons in 1972. He played four seasons with the Falcons before being traded to the Washington Redskins. He played for the Redskins for part of the 1976 season, and then was traded to the San Francisco 49ers for the remainder of that season. After his retirement in 1978, Sullivan went on to become a college football coach.

Position: Quarterback
Seasons: 1969–1971 (Auburn Tigers), 1972–1975 (Atlanta Falcons), 1976–1977 (Washington Redskins and San Francisco 49ers)
Born: January 18, 1950, Birmingham, Alabama

Dee Ford

Dee Ford played at Auburn from 2009 to 2013. Ford was on the undefeated 2010 team that won the National Championship. He was also a part of the team that won the 2013 SEC Championship Game. As a college senior, Ford was a First Team All-SEC selection. When Ford went pro, he was picked by the Kansas City Chiefs in the first round of the 2014 draft. In 2017, the Chiefs exercised the fifth-year option on Ford's contract. That means Ford will play for the Chiefs at least through the 2018 season.

Position: Linebacker
Seasons: 2009–2013 (Auburn Tigers), 2014–Present (Kansas City Chiefs)
Born: March 19, 1991, Odenville, Alabama

All-Time Records

4,327

Total Offensive Yards in a Season

In the 2010 season, Cam Newton set the SEC record with 4,327 total offensive yards.

12

Sacks in a Season

In the 2010 championship year, Nick Fairley led the defense with 12 sacks, an Auburn single-season record.

92

Career Field Goals Made

From 2014 to 2017, Daniel Carlson became an all-time SEC leading scorer with his 92 career field goals. He also holds 14 Auburn kicking records.

4,303

Career Rushing Yards

Bo Jackson had the second-best performance in SEC history with his 4,303 career rushing yards.

8,016

Career Passing Yards

Stan White is the number-one passer in Auburn's history, with 8,016 career passing yards. He was also the starting quarterback for Auburn's undefeated 1993 team.

Timeline

Throughout the team's history, the Auburn Tigers have had many memorable events that have become defining moments for the team and its fans.

1892
The Tigers play their first football game against the University of Georgia.

1893
The Tigers play the first-ever Iron Bowl versus Alabama.

1900 1920 1940 1960

In 1933, Auburn is a founding member of the SEC.

1939
Auburn Stadium opens.

1951
Ralph "Shug" Jordan is hired as the head coach of the Tigers.

1957
The Tigers win their first National Championship.

1971
Pat Sullivan wins the team's first-ever Heisman Memorial Trophy.

The Future
Head Coach Malzahn has been with the Tigers since 2013. In 2017, Auburn won the SEC West and narrowly missed a college football playoff. Heading into the 2018 season, the roster included promising talent with players such as returning quarterback Jarrett Stidham. In 2018, Coach Malzahn signed a seven-year contract extension and hopes are high that he will continue to produce winning football teams.

1985
Bo Jackson wins the Heisman.

2017
Auburn plays in the SEC Championship Game against Georgia.

1980 2000 2020

1979
Aubie the Tiger debuts as the university's mascot.

2010
The Tigers win the National Championship, and Cam Newton wins the Heisman.

Write a Biography

Life Story

A person's life story can be the subject of a book. This kind of book is called a biography. Biographies often describe the lives of people who have achieved great success. These people may be alive today, or they may have lived many years ago. Reading a biography can help you learn more about a great person.

Get the Facts

Use this book, and research in the library and on the internet, to find out more about your favorite player. Learn as much about him as you can. What position does he play? What are his statistics in important categories? Has he set any records? Also, be sure to write down key events in the person's life. What was his childhood like? What has he accomplished off the field? Is there anything else that makes this person special or unusual?

Use the Concept Web

A concept web is a useful research tool. Read the questions in the concept web on the following page. Answer the questions in your notebook. Your answers will help you write a biography.

Concept Web

Your Opinion

- What did you learn from the books you read in your research?
- Would you suggest these books to others?
- Was anything missing from these books?

Adulthood

- Where does this individual currently reside?
- Does he have a family?

Childhood

- Where and when was this person born?
- Describe his parents, siblings, and friends.
- Did he grow up in unusual circumstances?

Accomplishments off the Field

- What is this person's life's work?
- Has he received awards or recognition for accomplishments?
- How have this person's accomplishments served others?

Write a Biography

Help and Obstacles

- Did this individual have a positive attitude?
- Did he receive help from others?
- Did this person have a mentor?
- Did this person face any hardships?
- If so, how were the hardships overcome?

Accomplishments on the Field

- What records does this person hold?
- What key games and plays have defined his career?
- What are his stats in categories important to his position?

Work and Preparation

- What was this person's education?
- What was his work experience?
- How does this person work?
- What is the process he uses?

Trivia Time

Take this quiz to test your knowledge of the Auburn Tigers. The answers are printed upside down under each question.

1 In what year did Auburn win its first National Championship?

A. 1957

2 What kind of animal flies over the stadium before each home game?

A. An eagle

3 What is the name of the stadium where the Tigers play?

A. Jordan-Hare Stadium

4 What is the name of the annual matchup between Auburn and Alabama?

A. The Iron Bowl

5 Where did the Tigers play in their first bowl game?

A. Havana, Cuba

6 Which former Auburn star played both professional baseball and professional football?

A. Bo Jackson

7 How many Auburn players have won a Heisman?

A. Three

8 What is the name of Auburn's tiger mascot?

A. Aubie

9 Which NCAA division do the Tigers play in?

A. The SEC

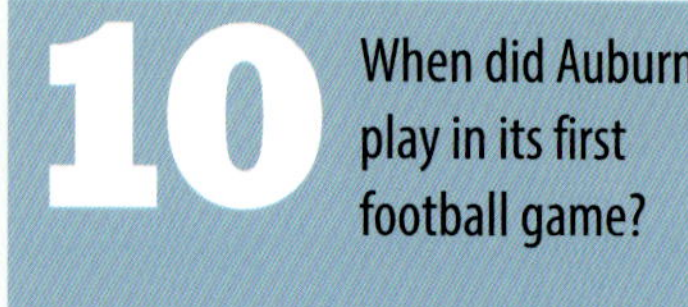

10 When did Auburn play in its first football game?

A. 1892

Key Words

bust: a sculpture of a person's head, shoulders, and chest

draft: an annual event where the NFL chooses college football players to be new team members

Hall of Famers: players judged to be outstanding in college football

Heisman Memorial Trophy: an annual award given to the college football player who best demonstrates excellence and hard work

Most Valuable Player (MVP): the player judged to be most valuable to his team's success

National Championship: the top achievement for any sport or contest in a particular nation

postseason: a sporting event that takes place after the end of the regular season

prominent: important and well-known

rivalries: competitions between different groups or individuals toward the same objective or goal

state-of-the-art: including the newest technology and features

Index

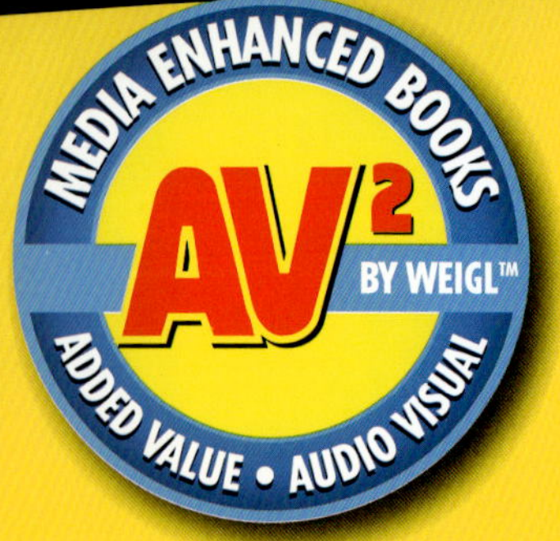

Log on to www.av2books.com

AV² by Weigl brings you media enhanced books that support active learning. Go to www.av2books.com, and enter the special code found on page 2 of this book. You will gain access to enriched and enhanced content that supplements and complements this book. Content includes video, audio, weblinks, quizzes, a slideshow, and activities.

AV² Online Navigation

Audio
Listen to sections of the book read aloud.

Book Pages
AV² pages directly correspond to pages in the book.

Video
Watch informative video clips.

Embedded Weblinks
Gain additional information for research.

Key Words
Study vocabulary, and complete a matching word activity.

Try This!
Complete activities and hands-on experiments.

Quizzes
Test your knowledge.

Slideshow
View images and captions, and prepare a presentation.

AV² was built to bridge the gap between print and digital. We encourage you to tell us what you like and what you want to see in the future.

Sign up to be an AV² Ambassador at www.av2books.com/ambassador.

Due to the dynamic nature of the internet, some of the URLs and activities provided as part of AV² by Weigl may have changed or ceased to exist. AV² by Weigl accepts no responsibility for any such changes. All media enhanced books are regularly monitored to update addresses and sites in a timely manner. Contact AV² by Weigl at 1-866-649-3445 or av2books@weigl.com with any questions, comments, or feedback.